# Faith of a
# Line Cook

## *The Gospel of Hope*

**"So, whether you eat or drink or whatever you do, do it all for the glory of God."**

**Corinthians 10:31**

# Brian Ingram

# Forward

*Generosity is not giving whats leftover, Generosity is giving the first bite. Generosity is giving when its uncomfortable. Generosity does not start once you "have it all". Generosity is born within our struggle. Generosity becomes alive when we decide to give regardless of our struggle,*

*Brian & Sarah Ingram Founders Purpose Restaurants*

All throughout the Bible, many miracles took place surrounding meals. Sharing a meal. Providing food. Multiplying food.

So many times in the Bible, words were simply not enough; miracles changed people's hearts and minds, spreading the message of Jesus.

Sometimes, God has us training our entire lives for an event that has yet to come. The only thing God is waiting on is for us to get out of the way and let Him into the driver's seat.

Every piece of my broken, imperfect life turned out to be the exact path I needed to be on.

Here is my story of the Hope, I have witnessed in my life over the last several years.

# A Dream...

In 2019, my wife Sarah and I dreamed of having a restaurant. A gathering place for good. A restaurant that would not only serve food but our community. We were both searching for purpose and knew our lives were meant for something more. How could we take everything I had learned from my 30+ years in restaurants and combine it with her love of people and heart to serve others?

The first step was, and always is for me, an idea deck. Dreams start to become realities once they are written down. My brother-in-law Eric has this amazing skill of taking the concepts I have in my mind and translating them into beautiful presentation that convey a message and feeling.

After the deck was finished, things started to fall into place. We found the perfect location: an old firehouse just a few blocks from our home. Hope Engine Company 3, built in 1876 by a group of volunteer firefighters. The building was scheduled to be demolished and was saved just in the nick of time by community activists.

Immediately, Sarah and I knew this space was perfect, and this was a project we were called to do. The next step was finances. At the time, I was the Chief Development Officer for a large restaurant group, and with my salary, we thought we might just be able to scrape enough money together to make this happen independently. We signed the lease, convinced my brother-in-law to help with design and marketing, and Hope was off the ground!

Not too long into the process, we discovered this old building was going to push back, and she needed way more love than we could afford to give her. I called a good friend and a previous business partner, Jeff, and pitched him our vision. An all-day breakfast joint that would give back a percentage of sales to the community. Without hesitation, Jeff said, "I BELIEVE in you, I'm in!" We were ecstatic, Hope was back in action! But the joy we felt was short-lived, as our world was about to come crashing down.

# You're Fired

My first call was to my good friend and real estate broker, Lonnie. I needed to figure out if we could get out of this lease. I had to find a new job and fast.

Lonnie was in shock and said, "Let me make a phone call. I know somebody that might be able to help you." Lonnie hung up, and after what seemed like only a few minutes, I received a call from a gentleman named Matt. Matt was an attorney with a local law firm, and he said, "Can you tell me what happened?"

I began to tell him I was fired for a non-compete clause in my contract. There were a million side stories, but I won't go into that here. That's a story for another time and place. I told Matt, "I have no money and no resources to pay you, and I appreciate the call." Matt said, "I understand, and I will help you!" Matt never wavered in this statement for almost two years. He stood with me until we reached the finish line. Angels are all around us, and sometimes they wear a suit and tie and identify as attorneys.

When this project first started, I had written what most would call a horrible business plan. This was a passion project; I just needed to break even and if possible, make enough to pay my wife and a dozen or so employees. We dreamed of having a safe and inclusive work environment for all; we wanted to give away profits, we wanted to give away food, we wanted Hope and Prayer Cards on every table, and invite our guests to share life with us. This was no business plan. It was a plan for disaster. We had a small 2500-square-foot dining room, a 250-square-foot kitchen, no storage, and a 140-year-old building that wanted nothing to do with our plans. How was this now going to not only serve our community but pay for our family to survive? How in the world were we going to finish this restaurant?

We had only one angel investor, our friends Jeff and Debbie, and they hadn't signed up to build a restaurant and support our family. Like every story you are going to hear in this book, they did so much more than we ever could have dreamed!

If there was a silver lining to getting fired, I now had a lot of time on my hands. Construction and clean-up have now become a family affair. We were the demo crew, the cleaning crew, we painted, we dreamed, and we prayed.

We were going to build this restaurant on a shoestring budget; we were going to buy whatever furniture we could afford, and chances are we might not make it across the finish line.

# God Kept Showing Up

It was late summer, and I had just received some chairs for our restaurant. The chairs we could afford came in boxes and had to be put together with about a million nuts and bolts. I was building chairs and putting the completed ones outside our large front door. I noticed a man standing across the street, and he kept watching what I was doing. I thought he must be planning to come back and rob us and take our new furniture and equipment. It kept eating at me, what is this guy doing? He would walk by almost every day. I had to find out what he was doing. I approached him, introduced myself, and asked, "What are you doing? I see you come by all the time." He simply said, "I'm praying for your business!" His name was Mick, and I discovered we lived in the same building a few blocks away. Mick became our guardian angel the next few months. He would call me when I left ladders outside, the front or side door unlocked, or just needed a hand.

Summer was coming to an end, and our free family labor was drying up fast. Our Son Ethan was going to be starting his senior year of high school, and our daughter Miya was headed back home to Idaho; she was living with her mom and finishing high school. Sarah and I were working nonstop, trying to get our dream off the ground.

Nobody liked working in this old firehouse late at night. It just felt weird. Our electricians told us stories of noises and events that made our hair stand up. We had all heard the story of Fireman Fred, who had given his life working at Hope Engine Company 3.

Ethan, our little super Christian, was having none of this talk. He had always had the gift of discernment, and it was time for a showdown. He had prayed several times over the building by himself, but this time it was going to be different. He went to a Christian school and had been leading prayer with his soccer team, so of course, they were going to come and have a prayer group upstairs at the old firehouse. They were praying for peace over our building. It worked! From that day forward, the space just felt different. The little issues that had been plaguing us were gone. Good things began to happen; people and miracles continued to show up.

7

My brother-in-law kept finding the most amazing craftsmen that would cost us half the price of any bid we had received. Their work was second to none, and all of them had a story to tell. Craftsmen who were taking their trades to a whole different level. Sign makers that hand-painted the traditional way, woodworkers that were transforming church pews into booths for our restaurant.

# The Tables Arrived

I still remember the call like it was yesterday. The man said his name was Robert; he had the most amazing accent that I couldn't identify where he was from. His voice was like healing water to my ears, and I can't come close to describing how it felt. He started to tell me his story, a story about his dream that was not going to be realized. He had dreamed of opening a restaurant, and now that was not going to happen. He told me he had the most beautiful tables made of copper, antique lamps, and velvet bar stools. The lamps had been shipped from other parts of the world and were very special to him. He had so many amazing pieces of furniture that he loved dearly. I kept thinking, when should I interrupt him and tell him we have no money for such things? I was waiting for the right time to tell him, to break the news. Then he said it. "I want you to have it!" I remember saying, "I would love to have it, we just can't afford that right now." He repeated himself once again. "I want you to have it!" It just wasn't registering with me. Was he saying he wanted to give it all to us? Yes, Yes, he was. Not only was he giving it to us, but he also had a company that was going to deliver it!

The day the furniture arrived, it felt like a dream. This beautiful furniture was here, and was it heavy! I looked at our 140-year-old stairs and thought, there is no way this furniture is going up those stairs. I have watched so many delivery drivers look at those stairs since this day, laugh, and say, "Not a chance!" I mean, not even attempt to carry a case of cardboard boxes up those stairs. I apologized to the delivery drivers and said I will try to find a way to get them upstairs; you can leave them here for now. The one guy said, "We got this." Two of the largest men I have ever seen put straps over their shoulders, then around the tables—solid walnut tables weighing over 1000 pounds—straight up the stairs. These guys carried pieces of furniture that never should have been possible up those stairs.

# Open for Business

We opened Hope Breakfast in September of 2019. It was a perfect sunny day, and Sarah and I couldn't believe it was happening! God had brought us so far, and we were more motivated than ever to give back. Our bank account was almost empty, but we knew we had to give away every dollar that would come in for our opening day party to Shine Bright for Cancer Kids. The Gospel of Hope was about to begin.

Here we were in opening week. I had gone from leading a large restaurant group with thousands of employees to working the egg pan at this tiny little restaurant. We couldn't afford a big team, so I had

my trusted friends and amazing cooks Marcia, Guermo and Elby working by my side. The amazing people became my lifeline. They cooked, they cleaned, they stood shoulder to shoulder with me every day, and some days they carried me.

My wife Sarah's years at Starbucks came in handy. Most days, Sarah was the barista, manager, hostess, server, and most importantly, my wing-man—my right and left hand, my everything.

God had been working double time while we had been building our little restaurant. He had been working on the hearts and minds of our community. From the first day we opened, the lines began. I was calling suppliers and getting food deliveries twice a day. We couldn't bring in enough food to feed everyone. This was a restaurant site nobody wanted; most would consider it a bad location on a tiny side road, a block off the main drag, with no parking and no hope of succeeding. The impossible was happening. They just kept coming! The media began to take notice, and it seemed like every day, someone was writing about us. From the day we opened, we never worried if we would make it. The problem was now going to be how can we feed this many people out of this tiny kitchen.

I remember my wife's face the first time I yelled across the dining room, "Stop letting people in! We can't take any more orders; we are out of food!!!" This happened again and again the first few weeks we were open.

The ministry of Hope was going to change the lives of our family, our team, and our community. Over the coming months, we held benefit after benefit, from Special Spaces for Cancer Kids to Zero Prostate, Blood Drives, and serving families in need. We were paying for funerals to Christmas presents. Our friends and family were working side by side with us to make it all possible.

# Covid Arrived

**HOPE COMMUNITY KITCHEN**

**WHEN PICKING UP PLEASE CALL (651) 330-8996**
WE WILL BRING YOUR FOOD OUTSIDE, PLEASE DO NOT ENTER RESTAURANT

In March of 2020 Covid was sweeping across our country, state and city, I woke up on a Friday morning full of worry and doubt. The world had changed in an instant, we hadn't been stock piling money for a rainy day we had been giving it out as fast as it was coming in. We weren't called to have a large savings account we were called to change our community. I walked downstairs at our apartment and began to pray. I cranked up some worship music in my headphones and asked god to take control, take control of my life, my business, everything. I once again had no answers, and no way out. We were low on cash and knew our business would likely be shut down in the coming days based off upcoming covid mandates sweeping across the country.

I also knew our community was in desperate need, schools had been closed. At risk Children across our community could no longer count on that one meal a day. I also knew if the children were not eating chances are the parents were not eating either.

My kids had always been filled with so much faith, even when I had none. They prayed about everything, for a large part of my life this drove me crazy! The prayed about the big things and the little things. I remember the day my son was asked to be captain on his soccer team. I was so excited, and he looked me in the eyes and said I haven't excepted it yet, I have to pray about it! What?? Like gods really going to give you a yes, or no? This was so foreign to me. What was it like to hear from god? Did he really speak to people? What was that experience like and why didn't I have that in my life?

This was going to be my morning! Something was stirring inside me; I had never felt the holy ghost on me like this. My mind was racing! The download was simple and so clear. God said we are going to have a story to tell, I knew what he wanted me to do! This was going to be a story only he could write and only a story he could bring us through.

GIVE IT ALL AWAY

# Give It All Away

As I sat on the couch, trying to process what God was calling me to do, I kept praying for a different answer. The same thought kept coming to me, and that was: no way out. In fact, it would probably push us over the edge. I had to give it all away. BELIEVE.

I took out my phone, pulled up our Facebook account, and just began to type. I simply said, "Any family in need can pick up a meal to take home at Hope Breakfast. The only question we would ask is: how many meals do you need?"

By Sunday, we had thousands of requests pouring in. I had to tell my wife that we needed to close our restaurant, our only source of income. I had no idea how we were going to pay our bills, let alone feed all these people. We needed to call a staff meeting and let our team know we were going to close to feed our community, and I wasn't sure how long we could pay them or if we would ever reopen.

We held the meeting. I cried, Sarah cried. Our team was so scared; they had families to feed and bills to pay. They were hurting, but what they did next forever changed our lives. Our team just kept showing up!

I went back to social media to spread the word.

CLOSED TO THE PUBLIC
COMMUNITY KITCHEN OPEN
FOR THOSE IN NEED,
SERVING MEALS 9:00AM -
2:00PM MONDAY - FRIDAY

Everything good in my life has happened over a meal; this has never held truer than today. Today, Hope Breakfast will stop operating as a restaurant and transition into a community kitchen. The next days and weeks are unknown. We don't know how we will be able to support not only our staff but also the hundreds of families in need. However, we will fight like hell to take care of as many people as we can for as long as we can. We look forward to serving our community in the only way we know how: through the power of a good meal. We hope to inspire restaurants around the country to do the same. We pray we can return to business soon and know the only way to get through this is to keep hope and support each other.

BELIEVE IN COMMUNITY, BELIEVE IN BREAKFAST

**Hope Breakfast Bar**                              ...
Posted by Brian Ingram
11 mins · 🌐

**At Hope we believe every child deserves breakfast... With all the school closings and our changing world if you know a family in need please have them contact us. Brian@hopebreakfast.com. We will have breakfast ready and waiting they can just pull up and we will bring them a takeout bag for the family. HOPE.. Help..Other...People...Everyday**

# The Phone Call

My phone rang and to my surprise it was Jason Derusha a news anchor in the twin cities. Jason said I have a friend with CBS national news named Jamie Yucas can I connect you. I don't know if Jason realizes that call changed our lives and that of our community. Jason's act of kindness to connect us changed everything when we needed it most. The power of the news., the power of humanity, the power of a story, has the power to change lives. He gave us a life line! It seemed like overnight Jamie was in our restaurant from NYC (CBS World News Tonight) and telling the world about Hope and the outreach to feed our community. Jamie told our story of Hope and Love, she took the time to listen, to share, to stand with us and to cry with us. Jamie even took time to ride around in a car and make some deliveries with us. Random acts of Kindness can change the world!

**Notes:** Hello I am a single mother of 5 who also cares for my mother who suffered a stroke and with the children not being in school I am struggling with putting food on the table for my family if you could help that would be a blessing than you so much

(Sent via *Hope Breakfast Bar*)

 **Brian Ingram**     12:25 PM
To: Jenna M >

Jenna you are considered and approved how many in your family ? We can have it ready for pick up at 3:30 today .

Please let me know if you are unable to make it and we will deliver to you !

All the best !


Brian Ingram
Owner
Hope Breakfast Bar

# When God Shows Up

It was opening day, operating only as a community kitchen; the team was almost all there. We all cried, hugged, and said, "We will get through this together." I watched our team, along with a handful of volunteers, work side by side. Some of these volunteers had nothing; folks low on money and resources were showing up day after day. They cooked, they cleaned, they answered phones, they delivered food, they handed out bag after bag, and if anything was left at the end of the day, they boxed it up and took it to homeless shelters up the street. These were people who couldn't afford gas to get to work, but they found a way. People who couldn't afford to ride the bus walked to volunteer. They just wanted to serve. At this point in COVID, almost no protocols had been set. Masks were in short supply, and they were being directed to front-line workers. None of us knew what we were doing, but we were willing to try.

Within a few days, we had emptied our shelves, our coolers, and most of our savings—and it was only day 3. Governor Walz made the announcement just a few days later: all restaurants must close to flatten the COVID curve. At that time, we all thought this might be a week or maybe two.

Within hours, my email was full of thousands of new requests for food, as hundreds of businesses were forced to shut down and thousands of families were left with no income.

I had no idea how we were going to feed all these people. I had a small line of credit with US Foods but no way to pay it back. I now know that God was using this season to challenge my faith. When you see no way out, you must turn it all over to Him. God had big plans, and He was in control!

## MIRACLES RAINED DOWN

Our phone had been ringing off the hook with calls from families in need, and now it was ringing with a community that wanted to walk with us—to stand with us! The calls went like this: "I heard what you were doing, and I have a car full of groceries. I'm on my way!" Restaurant after restaurant that had closed wanted to donate everything they had left in their coolers. Food vendors began calling: "Can you take a semi-truck full of produce?" Farmers began calling, saying, "I have a pig I want to donate!" God was taking this horrible situation and saying, "I have a way! Trust in Me!"

I watched in awe of our team. Phone call after phone call: "Yes, we can help. Yes, we can deliver meals. Yes, you can come every day if you need. Yes, we can deliver meals for the week for you."

# Change Was Coming

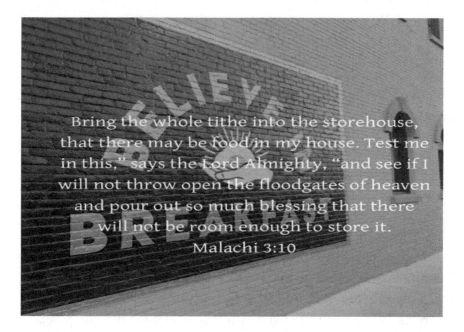

Bring the whole tithe into the storehouse, that there may be food in my house. Test me in this," says the Lord Almighty, "and see if I will not throw open the floodgates of heaven and pour out so much blessing that there will not be room enough to store it.
Malachi 3:10

I watched people who had never cooked in a professional kitchen slice thousands and thousands of pounds of carrots, potatoes, and onions. I watched them place wet towels over their heads; one day, it was ski goggles, hoping to prevent the onions from stinging their eyes. I watched as our cooks prepared thousands of meals per day, sitting on buckets and trying to snatch a minute of rest between meals. Most days, we didn't even know what we were going to cook. It was the real-life version of "Guy's Grocery Games"! We based meals on whatever provisions had come in the day before, and some days, it was whatever arrived that day.

Now, none of this was ever easy, but in the beginning, we thought we had this. Food suppliers had to clear out coolers before the food spoiled; restaurants were doing the same. Soon, the food being donated dried up. Suppliers had no more free food, and restaurants, which were closed, had nothing left to give.

The requests for food kept coming in—actually, they were increasing almost daily. In fact, the people who had been coming could no longer afford to drive to the restaurant to pick up food; they now needed it delivered. Requests from outreach centers that were serving some of the hardest-hit communities were now asking for help with hot meals.

I once again sat with my wife and said, "We have one week. We cannot go any longer; we have nothing left to give." It seemed that every time I lost hope, hit my limits, God responded and said, "I have a way."

The mailman became a saint. That news story by Jamie Yucas just happened to be a miracle. People across the country wanted to stand with us! I remember the first card that came in. It was from a child, saying he wanted us to have his allowance so we could buy more food for our community. Then another card arrived, containing the most beautiful story. "About a year before my husband died, he gave me this $100 bill. He said to keep it in my wallet and use it only in an emergency." She had carried this in her wallet for the last 5 years! This person gave us something that was irreplaceable. God was moving all around us! We began to gather as a group and open the mail—these amazing cards filled with encouragement from all over the country and the world! The message of hope was spreading! We would cry and say, "I can't BELIEVE this! How was this even happening?" God was moving in extraordinary ways.

Every one of the cards changed our lives. They were changing us and our community.

Thanks for all you're doing. Hope (well-named!)

About a year before he died in 2015, my husband gave me the Ben Franklin (inside this envelope), saying, Keep it for an emergency. So I've been carrying it around in my billfold over 5 years. (I think this time we're in qualifies as an emergency — and I'm grateful for your valiant efforts to feed our struggling neighbors.... .

# Hope Delivered

We struggled to fit meals into just our cars; the demand was so high, and we couldn't keep up. Then my phone rang, and my old friend Mark Palm called to ask, "have a food truck I can donate to you for a few weeks if it will help you?"

This truck became a lifeline, and not only for hot meals. We used it to transport donations of freezer goods that needed clearing out and dry goods that were close to expiration from warehouses.

Whenever one source seemed to dry up, God would reveal, "I have fresh water over here, and over here." Our delivery drivers became bearers of hope. I witnessed our friends and neighbors delivering meal after meal. One of our dear friends, Mick White, would bring his young son along on deliveries, affectionately nicknamed "Mack Mack Booty Crack." They were there every day, forging connections with the community and families in need.

Then, one day, a remarkable man of God named Mike appeared. Mike had been delivering meals for us multiple times a week with his daughter. However, on this particular day, he arrived with a new partner, his friend Topper, a local pastor from Eagan River Valley Church. My wife and I attended River Valley Church in Saint Paul, but we had never met Topper. His arrival was perfectly timed. The Spirit of the Lord emanated from him. He would enter, call you by name—usually followed by a hug—and then he would cover you in a prayer, much like a warm blanket on a cold winter night. He transformed lives!

**Winni Yin** 🔲 recommends **Hope Breakfast Bar.**

7 mins · 🌐

Dear Ms Sarah
Thank you so much for the wonderful foods you provided for us! I am Speechless! My kids enjoy everything you make for them! Last week they kept telling me they love hash brown and they love pancake and eggs, so that's why I come back to you guys again so sorry! We are so thankful for your kindness! God bless you Hallelujah
Winni

MOBILE COMMUNITY KITCHEN

# FREE HOT MEALS
# FOR THOSE IN NEED

EVERY TUESDAY, THURSDAY & FRIDAY
FROM 11:00 AM - 1:00 PM STARTING MARCH 26
AT URBAN VENTURES - COLIN POWELL CENTER

. . . . . . . . . . .

HOPE BREAKFAST BAR

×

CHAMELEON
CONCESSIONS

Like everything on this journey change was coming and this time it would be our food truck. It had to be returned and we were going to be stuck trying to load our small cars and SUVs . But like every time before God showed up!

I received a phone call from a gentlemen named Shawn. He owned a small real estate company appropriately named Pop Realty (people over profit). Shawn informed us they wanted to help us buy a new food truck. It seemed like only hours from when I spoke to Shawn to the day, we purchased our new Hope food trailer. God was still in control !

The needs for food kept coming but so did the emotional and social needs. We were watching on the news everyday of kids that were going to be missing out on so much. Proms and Graduations were being canceled. Students that had waited a lifetime for that one special night ! A time to dance, to remember and rejoice was not going to happen.

My wife Sarah and I decided we had to have a drive through prom. We had no idea how we would pull it off logistically or financially, but we knew it had to be done. We didn't know if kids would want to even do this? Would their parents even allow them out? So many families were in quarantine. People were scared and we just wanted to see people smile again.

# PROM NIGHT 2020

We devised a plan: to take as many kids as we could. We decided not to turn anyone away who wanted to experience a prom at no cost. We arranged for a band on the sidewalk, set up a red carpet with velvet ropes, provided flowers, and offered takeout dinner for all the prom attendees. Additionally, a professional photographer was present to document the special night.

The cars lined up along Grand Avenue, and our team members were dressed to the nines—looking spectacular! The police showed up to assist with traffic control. The kids showed up! They arrived in many beautiful ways. We witnessed mothers and fathers escorting their children down the red carpet. There were kids who had to maintain social distance arriving in separate cars, donning masks, and walking the carpet together, even if only for a brief moment. They picked up a meal to go, took a flower and a photo, said goodbye, and then returned to their respective cars to head home.

Limos arrived with kids who had quarantined together, and we witnessed smiles, laughter, and the finest aspects of humanity. Friends and neighbors on the streets applauded these incredible kids who simply wanted to attend and be acknowledged. Tears were shed, hugs were exchanged, and we thanked God for one of the most wonderful nights of my life!

# The Volunteers

Mr. Rodgers once said:

"When I was a boy and I would see scary things in the news, my mother would say to me, 'Look for the helpers. You will always find people who are helping."

If you ever want to know whether Angels are present, I promise you, they are all around you—people truly embodying the hands and feet of God. From the very beginning, we had volunteers who never worried about their own safety. They didn't care about money or recognition; they only wanted to help.

The stories are both diverse and yet the same. Immigrant families, receiving zero government assistance for their basic needs, simply wanted to contribute, to show up, and to feed their community. Marcia and Guermo remained steadfast; they braved snow and rain, driving 30 miles each way. Gato, our hero, a local veteran battling trauma and

PTSD, had already given so much and wanted to give even more. Local business owners like Tuffy, who had to close his family business, still wanted to help in any way he could, and he consistently declined a paycheck whenever we offered one. Our amazing staff of servers, bartenders, cooks, and support personnel kept showing up day after day. There were team members who had family members fighting deadly diseases like cancer, and yet they still showed up. They committed to going home and quarantining so that we could all remain safe when we showed up to cook and serve families in need at this small restaurant of hope.

# Hero's

Heroes were showing up every day, delivering meals, putting themselves in harm's way by arriving and leaving food on people's front porches. It didn't matter that we requested individuals to remain indoors when meals were dropped off; they wanted to express gratitude to the person delivering them. They desired to share a hug, to interact with someone. For some, this might have been the only person they had seen in weeks. This person brought a hot meal, and they wanted to extend their thanks.

Every single one of these heroes changed my life. By the time we were able to reopen, they had transformed hundreds of thousands of lives.

Everything was beginning to change, and we received news that we would be able to reopen. We could attempt to resume the business of serving food. We understood that many of the families we were providing meals for, the hospitality workers we were aiding, would still have needs. We realized we had to find a way to improve, to continue our outreach efforts.

My wife had always had the biggest heart I have ever known. From the day I met her, Sarah's sole goal was to bring smiles to people's faces. She'd act silly, sing, dance – she had a talent for even farting on command, which usually drew the heartiest laughter. Sarah had previously collaborated with nonprofits to combat issues like sex trafficking and prostate cancer (she had recently lost her stepfather to this terrible disease). Now, she was channeling that same passion towards battling food insecurity and aiding hospitality workers in need, by establishing our nonprofit organization, Give Hope MN.

If you've been reading this story and momentarily thought, "Oh, this Brian is a good guy," you're mistaken. My kids, my wife, my mom, and God had to work on me. They had to change me. For most of my life, I lived solely for myself, even though I had the best example of what it meant to possess a generous heart. I've observed my mom, as far back as my memory goes, helping those in need. I can't even recount how many times she rescued me from myself and my poor decisions.

# Redeemed

*Sometimes we must be humbled. Sometimes the shell must be broke to get to the good stuff.*

God needed to change me. I had been observing how Sarah treated people, how she showered them with love, how she selflessly gave everything to bring happiness to others. It was a moment that altered my life. Sarah and I were driving, and I had to take a call from a food supplier. I was so upset that the supplier couldn't meet our needs, and in my fury, I said terrible things to this person. Filled with rage, I hung up, and then my wife gently reached over and took hold of my arm. She posed a simple question, "What if someone spoke to your daughter in that manner?" It shattered me, in the best possible way, and I often share that story.

More than anyone else in my life, my wife has done something invaluable: she has believed in me. She has never said no – I mean never. She has always encouraged me to dream, to dream out loud and live my best life. God knew precisely what I needed most in my life, and He blessed me with Sarah.

**The People Lined Up**

We reopened our restaurants, and the blessings kept pouring in. Business had never been better. The city had granted us permission to close a road in front of our space, enabling people to be outside and maintain social distancing. Business exceeded our wildest dreams. We started paying off debts and began to dream.

The opportunity arose to acquire our second restaurant. It was a chance to take over an existing space, so it wouldn't exhaust too many of our resources, and we could manage much of the work ourselves. We jumped in wholeheartedly, with no safety net.

The world was undergoing rapid change. Covid continued to affect millions, and our city was about to be rocked!

# The World Changed

I remember watching the video of the George Floyd murder. It was horrifying to witness and even attempt to process the events taking place.

Our world changed in an instant! People took to the streets to demand change. Protesters gathered all around our community, standing up and advocating for change.

We observed our community crying out for change. We witnessed neighboring buildings engulfed in flames, and we saw our neighbors searching for healing. In response, we did the only thing we knew how to do: cook and feed as many people as we could. We drove into the cities to find anyone in need of a meal – protesters, National Guard members, and First Responders. God instructs us to feed all His people, and that became our mission. We observed, we prayed, and we shared a meal.

I distinctly recall the morning when I felt the presence of God. We had set up a table in front of Hope. The sign simply read, "Free coffee and food for all." I was conversing with an incredible family that had traveled all the way from Georgia. Parents, cousins, and children had all come to protest and lend their voices to the cause of change. I watched as tables filled with National Guard members, noticing a few police officers standing in the background. Their expressions were somber, their faces appeared empty. I said, "Please come grab a coffee and some food." They seemed as if they hadn't slept in days. Politely, they declined, saying, "No, it's okay, leave it for others who need it more." I insisted they come over, and reluctantly, they did. I witnessed conversations unfold between protesters, National Guard members, and police officers. I observed an officer offering an apology for actions likely committed by someone he probably hadn't even known. Their only connection was the uniform they both wore. I watched as tears flowed between them, as they hugged. I observed, prayed, and thanked God for that moment.

# Gnome What I'm Saying

**The one thing I have learned through all of this, Hope is all around us. You simply must be willing to see it.**

The day arrived for us to sign the lease for our second restaurant. The world around us was in turmoil, but for some reason, I had complete peace about moving forward with this project.

Once again, we had a shoestring budget, but we had a dream. We had faith, and we knew God would open doors that needed to be open and close the doors that needed to be closed.

Our first restaurant was an old historic firehouse, Hope Engine Company 3. Our second one was a 100-year-old firehouse, Engine Company 5 – another building constructed to serve its community.

When I say this old building pushed back, she pushed back hard. Every wall we opened had rotted timbers, pipes that were literally

56

crumbling in our hands, and old beer lines that stank so bad that smell may never leave me.

The devil kept showing up, but time after time, God opened doors. We didn't have money to replace the rotten floors, but we had Eric on the job! He found a high school that was giving up its basketball court, which would become our perfect flooring.

Once again, we couldn't afford much for furniture and decorations, but we knew somehow, someway God would lead the way. One day my good friend, Justin, called and informed me that Rosedale Mall had a food court with brand new furniture and games they needed to part with. We showed up, and they had everything we could ever dream of: large communal tables, high-top bar tables, dining room tables, chairs, bar stools, lamps, shuffleboard tables, pool tables – I mean everything! A furniture package that would have cost us two hundred thousand was only going to cost us Ten Thousand!!!

Some people may think we make our own luck, that this is all just a coincidence. I can tell you with 100% certainty God was in control and pointing the way.

We needed to move a bunch of oversized furniture and games up another 120-year-old staircase, except this one wasn't a straight shot. It had two turns; it was going to be impossible. As I stood in the parking lot trying to figure out our next move, I noticed a crack in one of our large bay windows. It ended up being a bullet hole. The Gnome had been hit during the unrest in our city, and one day a large group had gathered in the parking lot, and some shots had rung out.

Sometimes God takes what was meant to harm us and uses it for our good. See, this bullet showed me the way! Every piece of furniture we had bought fit perfectly through that window. We had to replace the window, which would require a lift and a window company. We were able to pull out the window, use the same lift, put in all the furniture, and put a new window back in.

# Winter was coming
# and
# A New Baby

The restaurant opened, and the response was overwhelming. We were incredibly busy, exceeding all our expectations. We managed to be open to the public while still serving our community. We provided meals for hotels functioning as shelters, catering to those staying with them. Public schools still needed hot meals, and by the grace of God, we were able to fulfill those needs. Typically, new restaurants struggle to make money in their first year; many can barely cover their expenses. However, we were profitable from month one. God was in control.

As summer was drawing to a close, concerns about a Covid-impacted winter were widespread. We took measures to ensure our continued operation. We invested tens of thousands of dollars in table dividers, patio tents, and private dining igloos for outdoor seating. We even acquired large fire pits, wood, and supplies to adapt for the winter season.

We expended most of our resources to prepare for remaining open during the winter, following Covid guidelines. But as had happened so often before, the rules and guidelines were on the brink of change. Restaurants were facing closure once again. It had only been a few months since we had opened. This felt too soon. We had just spent a significant amount of money to rent a large tent for our patio, setting up for socially distant dining. We even signed a tent contract for the entire winter. We were in trouble.

# More Than Food

Once again, we found ourselves at a crossroads. We were aware that the hospitality industry was on the brink of devastation. Many of the workers were going to have to wait for weeks, maybe months, for unemployment benefits to take effect. Necessities like food and toiletries – everything a family might require – would be in high demand. We understood the dire situation facing immigrant hospitality workers, including those from dreamer families with no government assistance. These were families left to live on the fringes.

We committed to transforming a tent that was initially intended to save our business into a tent to assist families in need. We understood that it needed to serve as a free grocery store, accessible to any family seeking to stock up on groceries, diapers, cleaning supplies, and any other essentials they might require.

On the first day, the line wrapped around our building. Despite the freezing cold, people kept joining the line. Our giant tent, which we had stocked, was full, and we believed we had enough supplies to last for weeks. However, just three hours later, the tent was empty. We had nothing left, and it was heart-wrenching to turn families away.

Sarah and I had exhausted all our favors with vendors, as free goods were no longer available. We had no clue how we could sustain this effort. We had filled shopping carts at Costco, thinking we had so much, but it barely scratched the surface of our community's needs.

During that week, local media once again started running stories about our message of Hope. Cars began to arrive, one after another, loaded with groceries. The Ramsey County Sheriff's department even reached out, saying, "We have more food than we can give out! We have partners that have given us hundreds of gallons of milk, produce, can you use it?" We were completely astonished. They continued to show up week after week, becoming a lifeline for us.

# Baby Banks

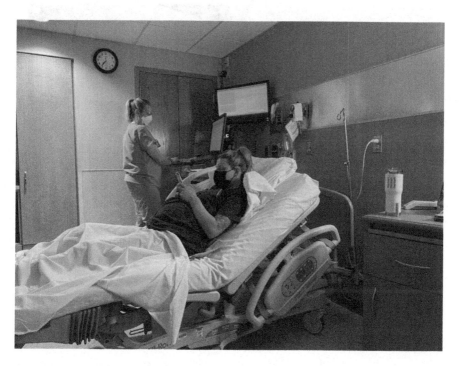

Throughout all this, Sarah had been pregnant. To say I was terrified would be an understatement. Sarah was close to her due date. She had been working and volunteering the entire time, and baby Banks was ready to make his appearance. The only problem was Sarah had just been diagnosed with Covid. We were checked into the Covid wing for expecting mothers. They wanted to get Sarah to the ten-day mark of having Covid before the baby came. Sarah began to struggle, our baby boy's blood pressure and heart began to struggle – he needed to come out, and he needed to come out now. It was like a horrible nightmare. We were not prepared for an emergency C-Section, but it was happening, and it was happening right now. In the minutes that followed, it was like the worst nightmare. Would Sarah be okay? Would our baby be okay? When baby Banks came out, he wasn't breathing; he looked so blue. Sarah had a curtain in front of her face, but I was watching it all. I thought, please God! Then I heard his little scream, the first cry. Sarah and Banks were going to be okay.

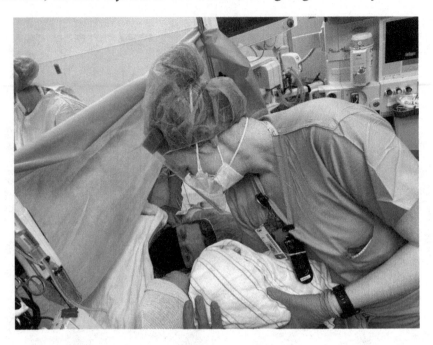

# Psalms 139:13-16 NIV

For you created my inmost being; you knit me together in my mother's womb. I praise you because I am fearfully and wonderfully made; your works are wonderful, I know that full well. My frame was not hidden from you when I was made in the secret place, when I was woven together in the depths of the earth. Your eyes saw my unformed body; all the days ordained for me were written in your book before one of them came to be.

The day we got to bring him home was going to be extra special since none of our family had been allowed to see him or Sarah. Banks was going to meet his family! Once again, God was moving out in front of us, opening doors and opportunities.

We wanted to capture this special time in pictures. Being a chef, of course, we had to dress him up as our little chef and take some photos.

Sarah's best friend is a professional photographer, and she created the most magical photos of our little chef. The realization hit me like a freight train. We needed to create a little chef calendar. We could sell this and raise money for our outreach! I sent the photos to a couple of my good friends and fellow chefs, David Fhima and Justin Sutherland, and within minutes we had a plan. Let's get all our fellow chefs in town to make a calendar and raise money for hospitality workers. Justin and David, in the coming days, had it all lined up – photographer, studio, chefs, sponsors, they did it all. Within days, we went from an idea to a photo shoot, to printing, to selling out of calendars. We raised thousands of dollars for hospitality workers in need. Within weeks, the first checks were going out

# Drive In

The holiday season was approaching, and the realization dawned on us that we needed to take further action. Our financial resources were dangerously dwindling, and we were running low on supplies. We wanted to give out turkeys for Thanksgiving, understanding that families grappling with food insecurity wouldn't even dare to envision Christmas presents. It was a moment to shift our approach once again. How could we generate income when we couldn't operate our restaurant?

Like so many times before, my brother in-law Eric and I started brainstorming. We should do a drive-in theater outside in our parking lot! We have a ton of space. We can buy some wood and build a giant screen. With absolutely no clue of what we were doing, we built it. How this giant screen going up 30 feet, screwed to a makeshift fence, tow strapped to a couple of trees and a few of our patio tent weights didn't fall over is a miracle in itself! Eric was the brains. He figured out how to get the movies legally and broadcast over the radio to the cars! We were now in the movie business and business was good! Each movie screening sold out, with an added perk: most attendees wanted takeout meals, popcorn, and beverages to be delivered to their cars. We were able to keep all our salaried managers working and keep a few team members employed!

# God's Plan

In the last two years of my life, God has transformed everything. Our small business of 12 employees has now grown to almost two hundred. We possess tens of thousands of prayer cards that have been completed, witnessing members of our team, who were as far from God as one can imagine, give their lives to Jesus! I have witnessed baptisms and seen lives being transformed. We have distributed almost 300,000 free meals and tons of groceries to families in need. We have been able to stand with families that have lost loved ones to violent crimes and assist them when they needed it the most. We have sponsored hundreds of Christmas presents for families that needed a lift. Currently, we are holding four Bible studies in our restaurants and are excited to witness that number double and even triple over time.

As I write and attempt to document this time of my life, this period in our history, it all feels so surreal. None of this is logical, none of it makes sense in the natural order. Why did God manifest in our lives? Why did He transform me? Why? I was so unprepared, so undeserving of any of this.

From the very beginning, I've understood that God had a story to tell, a story about BELIEVING. When all hope is lost, we simply need to BELIEVE and acknowledge that our God has a way, even when it's hidden from our sight.

God took a small, humble restaurant and a modest family and transformed us. He altered our life's course and demonstrated to both us and our community that miracles are still unfolding today. Jesus isn't just a historical figure from thousands of years ago; He's present even now. He remains the God of Miracles.

You only need to BELIEVE.

The lesson I've grasped through all of this is that God remains in control; circumstances can and will change. God utilized this season in my life to effect changes within me, within our family. The chapter of Hope Restaurants might one day end, and our purpose-driven restaurants could fade away. Yet, it will have been enough, more than Enough. I will forever carry gratitude for all those who stood with us: every volunteer, each family and individual who supported us, every business that not only stood with us but also uplifted us.

My children... Miya, my extraordinary warrior Princess, brimming with God's presence, possessing a heart unlike any other—a moral compass guiding me as I navigated my path to faith. You've changed me, Dad, in ways you will never know because I simply don't have the words to express. My oldest Son Ethan, you stand as a man of God, your manifestation of faith before the world's eyes has inspired me in ways I could never fully explain. You once said to me Dad I will have to pray about that. What profound words those were to me. Those words hit me everyday I need to pray about that. Dad is forever grateful for your example of leaning into your faith and placing everything in Gods Hands. Thank you for showing me how to listen to god.

Baby Banks, While you grew in Moms belly you were already changing me and our family. Your light in our world and that of our community was felt within days of your birth. Your smile, your laugh and hugs were a healing I needed and never knew it,

My wife, my rock. Sarah Ingram your a life giver in every way. You mended my broken self, you showed me how to give of yourself for nothing more than to see someone smile. I watch you do it everyday. You always want to make others smile even when you cant do it yourself. You breath life into me everyday even if your short on breath. I know that no matter where this world leads us we will be standing together and that is truly enough.

## I WILL FOLLOW WHERE THE SPIRIT LEADS

I am available.

Made in the USA
Monee, IL
14 December 2023

49325452R00050